Picked Apart the Bones

ISBN: 978-0-9797858-3-2

Chickasaw Press
The Chickasaw Nation
P.O. Box 1548
Ada, Oklahoma 74821

Printed by: Baker Group, LLC & Jostens, Inc - 405.503.3207

Design & Illustration: Skip McKinstry

Picked Apart the Bones

Rebecca Hatcher Travis

Chickasaw Press

I *Coils of Clay*

II *Listening to the East*

III Turtle Crawled Out

IV The Color of Pipestone

Biographical Note

Rebecca Hatcher Travis is an enrolled citizen of the Chickasaw Nation who was raised in the hills of Oklahoma. Her writing often reflects her Native American heritage and the natural world. Published work appears in literary journals, anthologies, Texas Poetry Calendar 2008 and *The Chickasaw Times*. She is a member of Wordcraft Circle of Native Writers and Storytellers, Bay Area Writers League, Gulf Coast Poets and the Poetry Society of Texas.

Preface

Picked Apart the Bones, like a slow growing pecan tree, took a long time to develop. The seeds were planted in childhood and earth, and blossomed with family and love. These poems hug the shores of the Washita River, cascade over Turner Falls, rise from clear spring waters within the Chickasaw Nation and sprout from the graves of grandmothers and grandfathers buried in Indian Territory. They are my stories and they are your stories. They belong to us all.

Author Note

In the course of writing this book, I have felt the
presence and encouragement of many ancestors.
I wish to thank my mother Lahoma, my aunt Doris
and my aunt Jenny for teaching me about kindness.

Coils of Clay

I

Coils of Clay

Gather at the feast in midsummer darkness
as moonlight weaves a snakeskin pattern
that slides over shallow river bottoms
away from long ago into this time

Take a bite of a history that screams
Remember! Remember!
then turn toward first light to watch a wildcat run
as she tracks fresh scent

Paws oozing into the soft bank at water's edge
along a high ridge
she climbs coils of clay
carefully pressed together

Layer upon layer
by one who knows her well
she runs, head down, in the blood
circling our dreamtime

Our medicine
better than any modern drug
this guardian
this spirit within

Picked Apart the Bones

Picked apart
the bones of Grandmother's generation
bones left baking in the sun

Gathered
bloodied marrow
the essence of memories

Wrapped
with care in soft supple skins
bound tight with strong cord

Carried
close to the heart
these ageless spirits

Now ride
in my dreams on fast horses
following the herd, chasing the enemy

They return
with heavy skins, winter meat
and daring stories to tell

Berries for Supper

In memory of Aunt Belle

She held her breath
dared not move
as the Indian Police hurried by
red dirt rising behind
thundering hooves

Crouching in the shadow of an old post oak
she cradled berries for supper in her apron
were they looking for Pa again?
they were always searching for someone
in the Territory

The last time the Indian Police rode to her house
a big man in a black hat said where's your Pa?
he sat high on a restless horse
reins held tight
anxious hooves stamped the ground just off the porch

He's not here she told the man
he looked at her solemnly then
yanked his reins to one side
and rode off as the group followed
and she slowly stopped shaking

Like steam from a distant train leaving town
their dust cloud trailed off down the road
Mama peeked through the window
little brother ran out the back door toward the trees
Pa was never home when the Indian Police came

Heart Full of Love

With a heart full of love
with a house full of children
she was raised to survive, to prosper
old ways left behind

Reaching adulthood
with children of her own
Grandmother ached to know
her heritage

Down narrow stairs in dusty archives
she sought her own family's history
but old traditions were lost
buried before her time

She gathered what threads she could find
wove them carefully into a warm red shawl
spread it over her children's shoulders
saying this is where we came from

Like a cicada climbing into daylight, taking wing
and finally singing arias he has long dreamed of
we step into the circle now, reclaim our culture
wearing her shawl with pride

Little Chief

In memory of Aunt Patsy

Chukma, little one!
just look at you now

Growing so big
my brown-eyed boy

Little Chief, you are
yes, miko iskunosi

You'll be a fine man
when you grow up

Be strong and brave
like the old ones

Here now, my handsome boy
come give Grandmother a kiss

Taken Charge

For those who seek burial sites

Now it seems as though
the Mother, the earth, has taken charge
and cradles them in hidden beds

Far from modern day memory
far from modern day eyes
stashed away with smiles

On their faces
ancestors
following the trail ahead

Growing Some Corn

Look at you
in your old lady fur
me in my old lady skin
just you and me, Grandmother
here for a short while longer

Come sit beside me
we'll be okay
spend our time together
growing some corn
to share with hungry crows

Seven Sisters Hills

In memory of Aunt Carrie

Native stone splits and crumbles
cracks and tumbles
into piles against collapsing walls
this old house is falling apart

An abandoned well out back
a sturdy barn down a well worn path
on this rolling allotment land
there to the north you can count the seven sisters hills

I step past sunbeams stretched out on the flooring
up in the quiet attic
searching not for valuables
to anyone but me

But for memories
keepsakes of another time
there, Grandmother's signature
carefully written inside a crumbling book cover

Scattered school notes, books, papers
lessons, photographs, boxes of handkerchiefs
a teacher's life here
leftovers in daily decay

Pieces of family I can hold in my hands
from an age now past
reminders of those who came before
and made today a possibility

Heading West

The wind murmured your name today
reminded me of your touch
your gentle ways
Grandmother
the wind said you sent her to speak my name

She whispered it into sweet wood smoke
circling upward over a growing fire
she shouted it aloud to lightning
playing hide and seek like a bashful child
at the far end of the sky

She lifted my hair
flung it across my eyes
as you passed through my heart
heading west
toward the dying sun

After All

Doggedly searching along Honey Creek
we finally discover her tracks in plain sight
waiting for us

She's up there in the rising hills
watching
after all

After all this time
after all the beloved mothers and blessed grandmothers
after all the clever daughters and cunning sons

In feverish visions
we still see ourselves
through the hungry eyes of the wildcat

Visiting

Visiting cousins in the countryside
told stay close, now, you hear?
searching through rock shards that form the road
to the house, suddenly a big brown hairy tarantula,
soldier of the field, marches right out in front of me
I'm a city girl, frozen in my tracks, but fascinated
I've been told they jump so I stand perfectly still
holding my breath, squinting in the sun until he's
under the barbed wire, into tall grass, out of sight
there's another strange stone, I scoop up the treasure
kneel down and fill my jean pockets until they bulge
with chips of red stones, yellow stones, white stones, striped stones
a hot blast of wind blows stinging red dirt in my eyes
so I step off into the grass and look down as fountains
of grasshoppers flee in every direction just ahead of my tennis shoes
spy a big black stone sticking out of the ground, put the side
of my shoe against it and flip it out, freshly unearthed
covered in damp red clay, the black stone goes home with me
at the end of the day

Legacy

Sweet earth
these allotted acres
his legacy, he said
for the ones to come

The land
how he loved
the land

With clenched fists
he held on
backbreaking years became a way of life

Against bare-boned walls
his shadow lean, bent and weary
he held on

Determined not to sell
determined not to lose
determined to pass on

The land
cradled by his gentle hands
Grandfather, imafosi

I, too
love this
sweet earth

Listening to the East

II

Listening to the East

Their whispers cling to the innards
flow through the blood
beat within the heart

Whispers of ancient times
when mounds were sacred
when the east brought life
and death was always close, so close

Their whispers carry us now
give us strength
in the shell shaker rhythm
in the circle of the dance

We hear their whispers
we know
the old ones watch over us

Coming

Silently slip through murky
waters on the great river

Watch the shore
watch the shore

Paddle slowly, ever aware
of sounds, of silence

Here, no twitter, no chirp is heard
step ashore, alert, on guard

Wary of intruders
who just keep coming

Cedar Smoke

She began so faintly
so quietly at first
she crooned again
her sorrow filled song
drifted through the gloomy trees

It circled their trunks
mixing with cedar smoke
in a dark dreadful time
her voice grew stronger
as she mourned her dead and wailed

Well Bred

Hear their galloping over the hills
ears bent back, tails held high
racing the wind, challenging the sun

Chickasaw ponies, every one

Don't you want to grab a mane
throw a leg up and ride
like our ancestors did?

Early Autumn, 1840

In a yellowed, handmade envelope
timeworn folds on written words
fluid strokes fading now
Dearest Mother, they read

My days are long
my nights unbearable
since Ben departed
to find our new home

He's journeyed west
where the prairie is wide
the weather more favorable
little Bennie can thrive

His letter traveled six weeks
I miss him so
he writes of green land
moist and mild

No bitter cold
Oh! The thought of warmth
no walls of snow to struggle through
in icy winter darkness

Yesterday in the town
a man grabbed at my bag
I'd rather take my chances
in a new land of our own

Ben says he'll make it back
by the end of November
I hope so
I'll be down to the last laying hen
by then

Winter House

Stand inside winter house
listen to warrior souls
rush by on spirit feet
they dart through the trees

as whispers of smoke
in the silence that follows
he waits by the fire
and sings a prayer for them all

Tree Loss

Our souls remember
how the people loved the trees
how they wept
tired cheeks pressed against familiar trunks

As they bid old friends farewell
how they mourned the loss of itti
and the trees they left behind
do any still stand today?

Remember This

We followed a trail of sadness
with heads held high
with heavy hearts
no turning back

No good to complain
bitter winds offered little mercy
frozen earth became
a sorrowful bed

Given no choice
we had to move
given no choice
we buried our dead

Down deep in this dusty earth
rest our family bones
the sadness lingers with us still
yes, we will remember this

Strange Taste

Raccoon tracks near the water's edge
rattlesnake skin on the trail
turtle hunts at a fresh water spring
we camp by a clearing at dusk
not much farther to travel now

Our people should be just ahead
we've come to this land of red dirt hills
river bottom valleys, prairies still
soon its strange taste will settle on our tongues
then we will call this place home

The Smell of Tomorrow

Somewhere in Indian Territory
she gathered old wood
to build her fire
against the aching cold

With the smell of tomorrow hanging in the clear night air
she considered this new territory
thankful for
familiar medicine

She looked to the sky and prayed
for courage
for strength
for the unborn child within

Sour Sweet

Frozen motionless in stagnant air
you watch them smile
white teeth gleaming
hear their honey talk, sour sweet

Come this way, now
we'll take good care of
everything
they coo to all who dare to listen

Then hurry off into decaying darkness
eager to chase after the next pot of gold
and you, like the wildcat, know to be wary
of the scent left behind

Bloomfield Blues

Now, child, don't sull up like that. Tell me, what's wrong? You're not eating, not talking, only thing you want to do is stare out that window. You work hard on your lessons and you never whine, but you're way too thin and your hair has lost its shine. What's bothering you? Now tell me, what's wrong? You're the first one here when there's mail from home. Are you homesick, child? Is that what it is? Now, wipe those tears away. There's just one more week until winter break, then your Pa will be here, sooner than you think! He'll bundle you up snug and warm in his buggy and you'll be on your way home for the long holiday. He'll come for you soon, you'll see, little one. He'll be here soon, you'll see.

Storyteller

Like a reflection facing us each morning
storyteller reminds us who we are
like sacred mounds shaped by the ancient ones
storyteller reminds us where we came from

Like beaded leggings passed down from Grandfather's generation
storyteller speaks of how we got here
as the guiding star that climbs high in a midnight sky
storyteller reminds us where we are going

Carrying our sacred traditions
storyteller speaks with the wisdom of the elders
and leans into the winds of the future
listening closely

Upright

Turtle, flipped on her back
strains to right herself
as we struggle to regain our history, our place
to right ourselves in this modern world

She bends a strong neck
rocks back and forth
tipping slightly side to side
barely making progress in her silent fight

As we work to gather our past, our bones
from curious collectors
museum back rooms and
musty archives

Her foot brushes the ground
fighting against the shape of her shell
as we battle against
ignorance and greed

Turtle claws her way over
at last!
she stands
four feet meet solid ground

Following in her way
we continue, we press on
in the struggle to stand
upright, feet firm on Mother Earth

Young Bones

Young bones carry the burden now
clad in suits and khaki pants
they bend under the weight tossed to them

Told here, take this
do what you can to make it just
our birthright, camped out here in the open

Downhill lie the secrets
perhaps you remember Grandfather?
his days in the sun were few

Yet council fires burn brighter before us
blazing far past the firelines, those invisible walls
for young bones carry our memories too

Turtle Crawled Out

III

Turtle Crawled Out

This old turtle crawled out of me
she's been waiting patiently

Gathering knowledge
changing, growing
keeping thoughts to herself

Now her voice is clear
her words appear

And the stories she tells
the stories escape
climbing out of their shells

Whisper

I must admit
the very first time I heard the singing
my heart galloped as if I had straddled a wild bucking horse

When I heard the rhythm
my pride swelled like Grandfather's smile

When I heard the shell shakers
somewhere a memory stirred as if

I knew these songs
knew this pride
knew this ancient way

Then I heard Grandmother whisper
dance

Honey Creek

I scramble beside a sharp embankment
below the waterfall
bare feet slide along cool water's edge
as my fingers seek a handhold amid the crumbling stones

In the instant
I find a solid grip
I hear the buzz
and every cell within me begins to vibrate

Have I stepped onto sacred ground?
soaked in serenity
the drone grows louder
a thousand waterfalls roar inside my head

And I realize
the millions of canyon bees that once lived along Honey Creek
are still here
living in memory within the beloved stone

Sweet Early Days

Perhaps you can see her...Grandmother tatting
on her living room couch
toe tapping as the kitchen radio
rocks to a modern beat

Spider threads twine through her fingers
that move as if she's playing her piano to a jazzy new tune
delicate blue circles hold hands
multiplying into graceful rows

My land, she says
as she sets her needlework aside
just look at the time
the backs of her ankles

Disappear into the kitchen
you hear pots and pans sliding out
of the stove storage drawer
clanging together in fluent pot-speak

Listening to the click, click, click of the potato peeler
you squint as a patch of sunlight
inches across the worn wooden floor
and crawls up the side of Granddad's easy chair

She whistles along with a song
tweedlee, deedlee, dee
tweedlee, dee, dee
you close your eyes and recall just how

Eye watering brilliant
the sunlight was
in those sweet early days
of youth

Like Fallen Leaves

Crisp oak leaves
leathered auburn like the work worn hands of elders
huddle together around tree trunks and stones
mingling with decaying brothers

On their journey, their return to earth
the heavy scent of this land saturates my pores
calling old memories out
hurrying up the hill an eager wind

Circles these headstones
while I stand here among my dead
breathing in so deeply
I hear the Washita below

Welcome me home
it knows this is my place
where I, like fallen leaves
will complete the journey and return

While crisp oak leaves hurry about
stirred by restless souls
listening to shaker shells and singing
in the blue mist valley below

100 Strokes

Your spirit sits with me now
when twilight deepens
into soft, quiet shadows
sits in the comfortable places you lived
content, hardly glancing my way

Serene
as you were
she brings a great peace
I ask her
to stay as long as she wants

Iposi, Grandmother, where you have gone
do you still brush your hair 100 strokes
and buff your nails to a shine?
your spirit sits with me now
but I cannot see her face

First Dance

I danced with my people today
to the shell shakers strong rhythmic beat

A fledgling circling within the dance
as natural as breathing, it seemed to me

I heard imafosi, Grandfather, declare
that one belongs to me

Yes, I am his and he is mine
although he has gone on

I danced with my people today
I heard Grandfather singing along

Kullihoma, June 2003

Full moon rises above Mountain House
fire keeper stirs bright embers
stacks more logs up, stirs again
around the sacred circle we gather

The young and the elders
the students and the teachers
called to this place, re-united
at peace with ourselves in this world

Singing voices rise together
shell-shaker rhythm, pulsing beat
old ways are held close here
Chikasha, we are, again, one

First Call

Wake me when the crows first call
as daylight grows
and a chilling wind sniffs around outside
searching for a forgotten entry

A neglected door, a warp in the wood
wake me when morning fires burn
and I will make us a tasty drink
to shake off the night

Then we can settle by the window
work in hand
to watch the crows up in the trees
summon the unused day

Crackles and Pops

Rows of glass panels block
blowing raindrops from reaching me
I want to rise up
fling open the door

Rush out into the night to greet the storm
feel the rain on my face
smell the world with a cleaner scent
welcome the gift with thanks

Sleep holds me down in a brotherly bear hug
whispers of dreams coming my way
I catch my breath at a flash in the window
and marvel as pure power bellows across the sky

Then flinch as the mighty storm
crackles and pops
and the blood in my veins
catches fire

Night Dream

Climbed out of the night dream
slowly
memory sharp as a fine whittled point
awoke to a rowdy crow calling my name

Dreamed of her again, spirit, smoke
holding my hand in silence
she smiled then whispered
you are of the old ways

And I remembered
turtle shells
sacred fire
and seed

Map in Hand

Map in hand
I drive out of town on a strange highway that twists like
a drowsy snake heading downhill toward a patch of sun
searching for something

To tell me I'm going the right way
there to the south like a mark on a tree
a sign turns me onto a two lane road
up a hill, down, up another hill, down

rolling over the lumpy backbone of this rural land
I rise and fall with its rhythm, destination up ahead
pass some turtles crossing the road
everyone has his own journey

The Color of Pipestone

IV

The Color of Pipestone

Sunset, the color of pipestone
drenches the world in burnt searing scarlet
tree frogs begin their pulsing songs in earnest
filling the damp air with their nonstop calling

Beseeching each other to come on over
on a darkening hilltop
watchful spirits ride on spirals
of sweet scented wood smoke

As faint remnants of pipestone
slice across the western sky
shell shakers stomp in rhythm
we follow their footsteps home

Whirlwind Dances

Welcome, wind
swooping across hilltops and down into river valleys, you
sweeten my days with the scent of
mountain forest, cedar and pine

Tumbling down onto golden grasslands, you
smack of tundra
and clear cold waters

Rolling along like a dry dusty tumbleweed, you
crisscross the desert, leaving
tracks on my skin

Blowing in from uneasy seas, you
carry slippery fog in your arms
to cool a feverish land

Your whirlwind dances up to me and carries my spirit off to play
I close my eyes, inhale
and greet the breath of Mother Earth

Secrets Left Behind

Anchored by the moon to keep the stars
from spinning out of control
night sky whispers of buried secrets
danger stretching out between her ebony arms
hidden mysteries gather inside rough canyon walls

Lonely shadows wander through hillside thickets
clutching secrets left behind by gasping young men
on blood moon nights in bitter cold wind
follow her signs and don't dare look back
night sky will guide you home

Stone Story #1

The ancient stone spoke

It told of primal birth
as a dazzling sunburst spreading light
above a wild raw horizon

It spoke of time passing
as the slow inevitable
erosion of a massive mountain dissolving into the plain

It spoke of great waters
frantic to spread as far
as they could run

And old earth
in her staggering beauty
fresh-scented and holy

Stone fell silent
then softly said
next time I will tell you of the people

Newborn Creek

Deep within the cross timbers
down a sunlit path
of startling reverence
I step into shadows of trees

So old they shaded my grandfather's grandfather
veer left at the fork and there
among a rise of huddled boulders gushes a fresh water
torrent as if Mother Earth squeezed

Her lips together in a perfect kiss
for those coming here to this special place
two butterflies dance on air
a matching pair, spiraling upward on

Moisture clouds in their act of discovery
they come to rest on golden stones
beside the newborn creek
wings spread wide

Savoring their blessed gifts
freedom of flight
a sweet sip of moisture
and warmth from the morning sun

Cricket Concert

Cricket sounds two notes
hesitates a moment, then launches
into full blown song

Filling the air with his wing singing
cranked up like big black speakers
at a rock concert

He plays on and on
showoli
don't your wings get tired?

Then he pauses
as if to check his playlist
for the next tune of the evening

Restless

The trees are so still here at night
not restless when darkness grows
like the trees in Oklahoma

There, they twist in the wind
as if their memories
cause them great pain

There, they bend and bow
to greet old spirits
resting at their feet

There, they dance and sway in the night
to the shells and the drums
of many Nations

But here, they sleep after dark
and rouse to the light
of the rising sun

Sun Swimming

A fiery sun slips off to swim
and dazzles us as he floats on his back
in bright shimmering waves
his blinding reflection outlined in salty golden foam
takes his own sweet time because, after all,
it's hot sweaty work heating this earth every single day
soon he shakes the water off, leans back
and slides over the horizon
disappearing in a quick slight of hand
before our very eyes

A Tender Place

The reason life ricochets off the trees
in this spot
why the air holds a buoyancy
and a warm fragrance
like the scent of home
soothes frazzled nerves

Why the morning sun skitters across
newly formed leaves
and beckons this creek
to sing its most beloved song
the reason is
this is a soft spot on the earth

Like the lack of bone atop an infant's head
a tender place, unprotected, exposed
stand here and listen slowly
so slowly you can hear the tap-tap-tap of woodpeckers
miles down the road
slower still when you can hear ants march as they move to higher ground

Slower until you hear squirrels leaping across
tree tops swaying in the wind
finally you will hear earth's heartbeat
steady and strong
its regular rhythm, you soon realize
is in sync with your own

Day Wind – Part One

This day wind wiggles his fingers in the dirt
rubs them together
then grabs hold and
somersaults across the body
landing lightly on his feet while he scoops up

Yellow petals of honeysuckle flavor
to scatter down the morning path
to sweeten the day
he blows with all his might to see
what he can move and what remains

While sweeping streets clean of persistent debris
he whistles and stutters
like old women banging shutters
through gaping barn doors
and between faded Venetian blinds

He rattles his way back and forth
careening through mountain passes
take care!
he sculpts drab desert sands
with strong muscled hands

Then abruptly stops and looks around
disheveled and panting
before scrambling up through the trees
blasting full speed across the flatlands
and finally dying down in some darkened valley

Night Wind - Part Two

While this night wind
flows cautiously
rolls over the skin slowly and deliberately
tasting the pores in small sips
sniffing in purposeful pleasure

She sails on hot summer sea breezes
caught after dark on oceans close by
and huddles in the shadows of January snowmen
collecting their ice for her children
the storms

After hurrying across patches of full moon light
she rests upon a bended branch
weary from constant travel
often whispering and moaning
in that old familiar voice

Sometimes she lingers
close to night blooming jasmine
which softens her blows
in the hours
before dawn

And when night rains fall
in sheets of dissolving drizzle
she disappears
in silence
taking the mystery with her

Old Bear Growling

Wizened as only an elder can be
old bear heard the hunters
though they crept carefully

Fleeing down a wooded ridge
he left tracks as he slipped across the creek
proof he had outwitted man once more

Holed up in a damp dark cave, he slept
fur soaked, stomach growling, dreaming of
warm meat, tender and sweet on his tongue

Keepsake

I would seal this moment
in a bottle
airtight, pure, crystal clear

Happiness and contentment
all too fleeting
gathered here

Acknowledgements:

The author offers grateful acknowledgement to the following publications, in which the poems listed were originally published, sometimes in slightly different versions:

"Keepsake." *Galaxy Literary Journal*, Edition III, Winter 2000 (107). Copyright 2000, Rebecca H. Travis

"Early Autumn, 1840." *Windows 2002 (30)*, Copyright 2002, Rebecca H. Travis.

"Kullihoma, June 2003." *The Chickasaw Times*, November 2003 (17). Copyright 2003, *The Chickasaw Times*.

"Remember This." *The Chickasaw Times*, August 2004 (13). Copyright 2004, Rebecca H. Travis.

"Listening to the East." *The Chickasaw Times*, November 2005 (12). Copyright 2005, The Chickasaw Times.